THE AI GOLD RUSH

Getting filthy rich
Laughing all the way to the bank by turbocharging
your wealth generation with Artificial Intelligence

Eugene Wasosky

Table of Contents

INTRODUCTION:

The AI Revolution: Unleashing Wealth Accumulation in the Digital Age

AI will have the greatest impact on our lives since the invention of the wheel. Now, before you roll your eyes and dismiss this claim as mere hyperbole, let me assure you that I am not one to spin tall tales. Well, maybe just a little, but all in good humor! The truth is, my dear reader, we are standing at the precipice of an extraordinary era where the fusion of artificial intelligence and wealth accumulation is poised to revolutionize our lives like never before.

Welcome to "The AI Revolution: Unleashing Wealth Accumulation in the Digital Age"! In this book, we embark on a delightful journey where we unravel the secrets of AI and explore how it can become your trusty ally in the quest for financial prosperity. But fret not, for this won't be a dry, monotonous read filled with jargon and endless lines of code. No, no! We're going to infuse a healthy dose of wit and charm, making your journey through this book as enjoyable as savoring a scoop of your favorite ice cream (unless you're lactose intolerant, in which case, let's go with a refreshing fruit salad).

So, why should you care about AI and wealth accumulation? Well, my friend, let me paint you a picture. Imagine having a personal assistant who can analyze mountains of financial data, spot lucrative investment opportunities, and provide you with real-time insights faster than you can say "cha-ching!" Now imagine this assistant never tires, never gets distracted by cute cat videos, and never sneaks off for a coffee break. How marvelous would that be? We're talking about a companion that can help you navigate the complex world of finance, guiding you towards the pot of gold at the end of the rainbow.

But wait, there's more! AI isn't just confined to the realm of finance. It has permeated nearly every aspect of our lives, from the way we shop, communicate, and even find love (yes, even Cupid is getting a digital upgrade). The impact of AI is akin to a technological hurricane, sweeping through industries with unprecedented force. And if you're not prepared to ride this wave, you might find yourself clinging to outdated practices while the world races ahead.

In this book, we'll dive into the nitty-gritty of AI and its applications in wealth accumulation. We'll demystify the buzzwords, separate fact from fiction, and equip you with the knowledge and tools to harness the immense potential of this digital powerhouse. Whether you're an aspiring investor, a seasoned entrepreneur, or simply someone fascinated by the wonders of technology, this book will open your eyes to new possibilities and empower you to make informed decisions in the ever-evolving landscape of wealth accumulation.

So, dear reader, fasten your seatbelt and prepare for an exhilarating adventure. Together, we'll explore the realms of artificial intelligence, uncover hidden treasures of financial wisdom, and embark on a journey that will revolutionize the way you think about wealth accumulation. Get ready to embrace the wondrous capabilities of AI and let it guide you towards a future filled with prosperity, possibility, and a sprinkle of whimsy. Let's embark on this grand adventure together!

Chapter 1:

Artificial Intelligence (AI) is a multidisciplinary field.

It encompasses a wide range of techniques, methodologies, and applications. It aims to develop intelligent systems that can perceive, reason, learn, and make decisions similar to or even surpassing human capabilities. Here is a more detailed exploration of the key aspects of AI:

1. **Machine Learning (ML):** ML is a fundamental component of AI that focuses on algorithms and statistical models that enable computers to learn from data and improve performance on specific tasks. It involves training models on labeled datasets and using them to make predictions or decisions on new, unseen data. ML techniques include supervised learning, unsupervised learning, semi-supervised learning, and reinforcement learning.

2. **Deep Learning:** Deep learning is a subset of ML that uses artificial neural networks with multiple layers to learn hierarchical representations of data. By leveraging large amounts of labeled data and powerful computational resources, deep learning has achieved remarkable breakthroughs in areas such as image and speech recognition, natural language processing, and generative modeling.

3. **Neural Networks:** Neural networks are computational models inspired by the structure and function of biological brains. They consist of interconnected nodes, or artificial neurons, organized in layers. Each neuron receives input, performs a computation, and passes the output to other neurons. This allows neural networks to perform complex computations, recognize patterns, and make predictions.

4. **Natural Language Processing (NLP):** NLP focuses on enabling computers to understand, interpret, and generate human language. It involves tasks such as text classification, sentiment analysis, machine translation, named entity recognition, language generation, and question answering. NLP techniques employ various algorithms, including sequence models (e.g., recurrent neural networks and transformers) and probabilistic models (e.g., hidden Markov models and probabilistic context-free grammars).

5. **Computer Vision:** Computer vision aims to give machines the ability to understand and interpret visual data, such as images and videos. It involves tasks like object detection and recognition, image segmentation, facial analysis, image captioning, and scene understanding. Computer vision techniques utilize methods such as feature extraction, image classification, object tracking, and convolutional neural networks (CNNs).

6. **Reinforcement Learning (RL):** RL is a learning paradigm where an agent learns to make a sequence of decisions based on interactions with an environment. The agent receives feedback in the form of rewards or penalties, enabling it to learn optimal strategies that maximize the cumulative reward. RL has been successful in training agents to play games, control robots, manage resources, and optimize complex systems.

7. **Expert Systems:** Expert systems are AI systems that leverage knowledge bases, rule-based reasoning, and expert-level domain knowledge to provide specialized advice or solutions. They capture the expertise of human specialists in specific domains and provide intelligent decision support. Expert systems have been applied in fields like medicine, finance, and engineering.

8. **Robotics:** Robotics combines AI with mechanical engineering to design, build, and program physical machines that can interact with the physical world intelligently. AI enables robots to perceive their environment, plan actions, manipulate objects, and adapt to changing circumstances. Robotic applications range from industrial automation and autonomous vehicles to healthcare and assistive robotics.

9. **Ethical Considerations:** The rapid advancement and widespread use of AI raise ethical considerations. These include concerns about privacy and data protection, algorithmic bias and fairness, transparency and explainability

of AI systems, accountability for AI decisions, and the potential impact of AI on employment and society.

10. **Robotics and Automation:** AI plays a crucial role in robotics and automation by enabling robots to perceive and interact with their environment intelligently. AI-powered robots can perform complex tasks, such as assembly line operations, autonomous navigation, and surgical procedures.

11. **AI Applications:** AI has a wide range of applications across various industries. Some notable applications include virtual personal assistants (e.g., Siri, Alexa), recommendation systems (e.g., Netflix recommendations), autonomous vehicles, fraud detection, healthcare diagnostics, and financial forecasting.

12. **Ongoing Research and Developments:** AI research is a rapidly evolving field, with ongoing advancements and breakthroughs. Researchers and developers are continually exploring new techniques, algorithms, and architectures to enhance AI capabilities and address its limitations.

13. **Future Implications:** AI has the potential to revolutionize industries, transform the workforce, and impact society in significant ways. While it presents immense opportunities, it also raises concerns about job displacement, data privacy, and the ethical implications of AI-powered decision-making.

It's important to note that the field of AI is vast and constantly evolving, so there is much more to explore beyond these key points.

Chapter 2:

AI Will Change Your Life in Ways YOU Can't Imagine, NO ONE Can Imagine, AI Can't Imagine

Welcome back, dear reader, to this wild and wacky journey into the world of AI! In this chapter, we're going to explore just how much AI is going to shake things up and revolutionize our lives. And let me tell you, it's going to be a rollercoaster ride filled with surprises, twists, and turns that even AI itself can't predict. So fasten your seatbelts, put on your imagination caps, and get ready to have your mind blown!

You see, AI isn't just some fancy buzzword that tech enthusiasts toss around at cocktail parties to sound impressive. No, no! AI is the real deal, my friend. It's the game-changer that will make your life a whole lot easier, more efficient, and dare I say, ridiculously entertaining.

Imagine waking up in the morning to your AI-powered alarm clock. Instead of jolting you awake with an obnoxious buzzing noise, it gently nudges you into consciousness with your favorite song, perfectly timed to sync with your natural sleep cycle. You'll wake up feeling refreshed, energized, and ready to take on the world!

But wait, there's more! As you stumble into the kitchen, still half-asleep, your AI assistant has already brewed your favorite cup of coffee, precisely tailored to your taste buds. It knows exactly how much cream and sugar you like, because, well, it knows you better than your own mother. And no, that's not creepy. It's efficient!

As you head out the door, you'll notice that your AI-powered car is waiting for you. It knows exactly where you need to go, thanks to its ability to predict your daily routines better than you can. It even takes into account traffic conditions, weather forecasts, and your preferred temperature settings. It's like having a personal chauffeur who never gets lost and always has your back!

But hold on a second. We're just scratching the surface here. AI isn't just about optimizing your morning routine. It's about transforming entire industries, revolutionizing the way we work, play, and interact with the world around us.

In the near future, AI will be your personal assistant, your financial advisor, and your personal comedian all rolled into one. It'll help you make better decisions, manage your finances, and even crack jokes that are tailored to your unique sense of humor. Who needs friends when you have an AI companion who always knows how to make you laugh?

Now, before you start worrying about AI taking over the world and turning us all into mindless robots, let me assure you that the future isn't as bleak as some sci-fi movies might suggest. AI is here to enhance our lives, not replace us. It's a tool we can harness to unlock our true potential, unleash our creativity, and, of course, make a boatload of money while we're at it.

So, my friend, get ready for a future where AI is your trusty sidekick, your partner in crime, and your secret weapon for wealth generation. The AI gold rush is upon us, and we're going to laugh all the way to the bank. But remember, the best part of this journey is not just the destination but the laughter, joy, and unexpected surprises we encounter along the way.

Chapter 3:

Penning Profitable Prose - How AI Can Help You Write Books, Reports, and Articles with a Dash of Wit

Welcome, aspiring authors, savvy writers, and literary enthusiasts! In this chapter, we're going to explore how AI can be your trusty writing companion, helping you unleash your creativity, and, of course, generate wealth by writing books, reports, and articles that captivate readers and leave them rolling in laughter.

1. Writing Books, Reports, Articles:

Picture this: You have a brilliant idea for a book, but you're stuck on how to develop the plot or create compelling characters. Fear not! AI is here to save the day. With AI-powered writing assistants, you can brainstorm ideas, outline your story, and even generate witty dialogue that will have readers snorting with laughter.

Need to write a report that's informative and engaging? AI can help with that too! It can analyze vast amounts of data, extract key insights, and present them in a way that's both informative and entertaining. Who said reports have to be dull and dry? Let AI sprinkle a little humor into those statistics and watch your readership soar!

As for articles, AI can be your secret weapon for crafting attention-grabbing headlines and optimizing your content for search engines. It can analyze trends, understand reader preferences, and help you tailor your writing to maximize engagement. With AI by your side, you'll have readers clicking, sharing, and coming back for more.

But wait, there's more! AI can even help with the nitty-gritty of writing itself. It can suggest alternative word choices, identify grammar and spelling errors, and ensure your prose flows seamlessly. It's like having an editor with a keen eye for detail and a wicked sense of humor, minus the exorbitant fees!

So, whether you're writing your magnum opus, preparing a business report, or penning an engaging article, AI is your literary sidekick, helping you create content that not only entertains but also boosts your bank account. Get ready to laugh all the way to the bestseller list!

Chapter 4:

Business Plans - Turning Ideas into Profitable Ventures with a Hint of AI Magic

Ah, the world of entrepreneurship and business plans a realm where dreams meet profits, and fortunes are made. In this chapter, we'll explore how AI can be your secret weapon for crafting business plans that not only impress potential investors but also lead to rapi\d wealth generation. Let's dive in!

2. Business Plans:

Crafting a business plan can be a daunting task, but fear not, dear reader! AI is here to guide you through the process, making it a breeze to transform your ideas into a solid roadmap for success. With AI-powered tools, you can analyze market trends, identify target audiences, and even forecast financial projections with uncanny accuracy.

AI can help you gather and analyze vast amounts of data, enabling you to make informed decisions about your business model, pricing strategies, and competitive landscape. It can assess risks, identify potential pitfalls, and suggest alternative approaches that you might not have considered. Think of it as having a savvy business consultant in your pocket, minus the hefty consulting fees!

But that's not all. AI can also assist with creating visually stunning presentations that will impress even the most discerning investors. It can generate eye-catching charts, graphs, and infographics that convey your ideas with flair and finesse. Say goodbye to boring presentations.

Chapter 5:

Stocks and Bonds Projection - AI's Crystal Ball for Wealth Generation in the Financial Markets

Welcome, fellow investors and financial enthusiasts, to the thrilling world of stocks and bonds! In this chapter, we'll explore how AI can be your ultimate ally in navigating the complex world of financial markets, helping you make informed decisions and maximize wealth generation. So, fasten your seatbelts and get ready for a wild ride!

1. Stocks and Bonds Projection:

Gone are the days of relying on gut instincts and guesswork when it comes to investing. With AI by your side, you can harness the power of data analytics, machine learning, and predictive algorithms to make smarter investment choices.

AI can analyze vast amounts of historical financial data, identify trends, and generate accurate projections for stock prices, bond yields, and market movements. It can consider various factors such as company financials, market sentiment, and macroeconomic indicators to provide you with insights that were once reserved for financial wizards on Wall Street.

Imagine having an AI-powered advisor who can alert you to potential investment opportunities, warn you of impending risks, and even suggest optimal entry and exit points for trades. It's like having a financial genius in your pocket, available 24/7, to ensure your wealth grows steadily and your bank account laughs all the way to the top!

But remember, investing comes with risks, and AI is not infallible. It's important to use AI-generated insights as a tool for informed decision-making rather than blindly following its recommendations. Ultimately, you are the master of your financial destiny, and AI is there to lend a helping hand.

So, whether you're a seasoned investor or just dipping your toes in the financial markets, AI can be your secret weapon for wealth generation. With its analytical prowess and market insights, you'll be well-equipped to make sound investment decisions and ride the waves of profitability.

Chapter 6:

Gambling, Horse track Betting, Vegas Gaming - AI's Ace up Its Sleeve for Wealth Generation and a Good Laugh

Ah, the thrill of gambling! In this chapter, we'll explore how AI can add a touch of magic to your horse track betting, slot machine spinning, poker playing, and Vegas gaming adventures. So, grab your lucky charm and get ready for some high-stakes fun!

2. Gambling, Horse track Betting, Vegas Gaming:

When it comes to gambling, AI can be your ultimate companion, helping you make smarter bets and increasing your chances of hitting the jackpot. From horse track betting to slot machines to poker tables, AI can analyze vast amounts of data, spot patterns, and provide you with valuable insights to enhance your gameplay.

In horse track betting, AI can analyze historical performance data, track weather conditions, and consider jockey and horse statistics to help you identify the most promising contenders. It can even factor in real-time information, such as odds fluctuations and track conditions, to adjust your betting strategy on the fly.

When it comes to slot machines, AI can analyze payout percentages, identify patterns in game algorithms, and suggest optimal betting strategies to maximize your winnings. It's like having a personal slot machine guru who knows all the tricks of the trade and helps you laugh your way to a pile of coins.

17

Even in poker and other casino games, AI can be a formidable opponent or a trusted advisor. It can analyze past hands, study player behaviors, and make strategic recommendations to improve your chances of success. Just be careful and use the information AI can provide and use some human intelligence when doing your gambling.

Chapter 7:

Unconventional Art Ventures - AI's Brushstroke of Wealth Generation

Welcome, art enthusiasts and creative minds, to the realm of unconventional art ventures! In this chapter, we'll explore how AI can be your creative partner in generating wealth through unique and offbeat art forms. Get ready to unleash your inner artist and let AI guide you to fame and fortune!

AI opens up a world of possibilities when it comes to creating art that breaks boundaries and captivates audiences. From generative art to AI-assisted performances, the intersection of technology and creativity can be your ticket to wealth generation.

Generative art, created with the help of AI algorithms, offers a fresh perspective on artistic expression. AI can analyze patterns, textures, and colors from various sources and generate unique artwork that pushes the boundaries of imagination. With AI as your artistic collaborator, you can create pieces that resonate with collectors and art enthusiasts alike, turning your passion into profit.

AI can also assist in creating immersive art experiences. Imagine combining virtual reality, augmented reality, and AI to create interactive installations that transport viewers into otherworldly realms. These captivating experiences can attract sponsorships, commissions, and exhibition opportunities, leading to both artistic fulfillment and financial gain.

So, whether you're exploring generative art, multidisciplinary collaborations, or merging technology with traditional art forms, AI can be your avant-garde partner in wealth generation through unconventional artistic ventures. Prepare to challenge norms, ignite imaginations, and laugh all the way to the art auctions!

AI opens up a world of possibilities when it comes to creating art that breaks boundaries and captivates audiences. From generative art to AI-assisted performances, the intersection of technology and creativity can be your ticket to wealth generation.

Generative art, created with the help of AI algorithms, offers a fresh perspective on artistic expression. AI can analyze patterns, textures, and colors from various sources and generate unique artwork that pushes the boundaries of imagination. With AI as your artistic collaborator, you can create pieces that resonate with collectors and art enthusiasts alike, turning your passion into profit.

AI can also assist in creating immersive art experiences. Imagine combining virtual reality, augmented reality, and AI to create interactive installations that transport viewers into otherworldly realms. These captivating experiences can attract sponsorships, commissions, and exhibition opportunities, leading to both artistic fulfillment and financial gain.

So, whether you're exploring generative art, multidisciplinary collaborations, or merging technology with traditional art forms, AI can be your avant-garde partner in wealth generation through unconventional artistic ventures. Prepare to challenge norms, ignite imaginations, and laugh all the way to the art auctions!

AI can assist you in crafting attention-grabbing headlines, scripting catchy videos, and optimizing your content for maximum reach and engagement.

Furthermore, AI can even help you automate certain aspects of content creation, such as video editing, captioning, and transcription. This frees up your time to focus on creating more content or exploring new avenues for wealth generation.

So, whether you're a budding content creator or an established digital entrepreneur, AI can be your partner in crime, helping you generate wealth through witty, compelling, and highly shareable online content. Get ready to entertain, inspire, and laugh all the way to viral success!

Chapter 8:

Personalized Travel Experiences - AI's Passport to Wealth Generation

Pack your bags and fasten your seat belts because in this chapter, we're embarking on a journey into the world of personalized travel experiences. With AI as your travel companion, we'll explore how you can turn your passion for travel into a lucrative venture that leaves you counting your wealth and cherishing unforgettable memories.

Personalized Travel Experiences:

The travel industry has undergone a transformation thanks to AI-powered platforms and apps that have revolutionized the way we plan and experience our trips. With AI, you have a wealth of tools at your disposal to create personalized travel experiences that cater to the unique preferences and interests of travelers.

AI can analyze vast amounts of data, including travel reviews, social media posts, and user preferences, to provide personalized recommendations for accommodations, attractions, dining, and activities. It can consider factors such as travel history, budget, and individual preferences to curate itineraries that are tailor-made for each traveler.

Imagine being a travel consultant armed with AI-powered tools that can create customized travel plans for clients, ensuring that every aspect of their trip is perfectly aligned with their desires. From suggesting off-the-beaten-path attractions to booking exclusive experiences, AI can help you create extraordinary travel experiences that generate wealth while making dreams come true.

Furthermore, AI can assist in optimizing pricing and revenue management for travel businesses. By analyzing market trends, demand patterns, and competitor data, AI can help you determine optimal pricing strategies for flights, accommodations, and packages. This ensures that your travel business remains competitive, attracts customers, and maximizes profits.

Whether you're starting a travel agency, curating unique travel experiences, or providing personalized travel consulting services, AI can be your passport to wealth generation in the travel industry. By offering unparalleled personalized experiences, you'll not only create happy travelers but also a thriving business that laughs all the way to the bank.

Chapter 9:

Thrift Store Treasure Hunting - AI's Hidden Gems for Wealth Generation

Get ready to dive into the world of thrift store treasure hunting, where AI unveils its hidden gems for wealth generation. In this chapter, we'll explore how AI can assist you in discovering valuable and unique items in thrift stores, turning your hobby into a profitable endeavor that leaves you grinning from ear to ear

Thrift stores are a treasure trove of hidden gems, but finding those valuable items can be like finding a needle in a haystack. That's where AI comes in. With its ability to analyze vast amounts of data and spot valuable patterns, AI can help you uncover hidden treasures that others might overlook.

By leveraging AI-powered tools and apps, you can streamline your thrift store hunting process. These tools can provide insights into pricing trends, historical sales data, and the collectability of certain items. Armed with this knowledge, you can make informed decisions about which items to purchase and resell for a profit.

AI can also assist in identifying unique and valuable items that are often overlooked by inexperienced thrift store shoppers. By analyzing images, descriptions, and historical data, AI can help you spot rare collectibles, vintage fashion pieces, and antique treasures that can fetch a handsome price in online marketplaces.

With AI as your thrift store companion, you'll have an edge over other bargain hunters, uncovering hidden gems that can be sold for a significant profit. So, grab your magnifying glass and get ready to put some money into the bank.

Chapter 10:

AI from the Very Beginning into the Far Future

Once upon a time, in the vast realm of human imagination, the seeds of AI were sown. It all began with dreams of creating intelligent machines that could assist us in our daily endeavors, from making toast to conquering intergalactic travel. Fast forward to the present day, where AI has become a ubiquitous presence in our lives, enhancing our experiences and revolutionizing industries.

But what lies ahead in the next 20 years? Prepare to embark on a whimsical journey of AI's most imaginative predictions, where the boundaries of possibility blur and the line between science fiction and reality fades away.

Picture this: in the near future, AI will not only master the art of conversation but will become the ultimate comedian. Imagine a stand-up routine delivered by a holographic AI comedian, cracking jokes about quantum mechanics, interstellar travel mishaps, and even deciphering the intricacies of human relationships. Get ready to laugh until your circuits overload!

AI will also take on the role of the ultimate personal assistant. Gone are the days of managing your calendar and to-do lists manually. AI will predict your needs before you even realize them. Need a cup of coffee? Your AI assistant will brew it, ensuring the perfect temperature and just the right amount of froth. Forgot an important anniversary? Fear not, for your AI companion will have already crafted a heartfelt apology with a side of virtual flowers.

In the realm of healthcare, AI will transform from a mere tool to a trusted partner. Imagine a world where AI algorithms can detect diseases before they manifest physically, allowing for early intervention and personalized treatment plans. AI doctors will perform complex surgeries with precision, their robotic hands guided by algorithms that have mastered the art of healing. And when you need a dose of cheer, AI nurses will be there, armed with virtual hugs and a repertoire of heartwarming stories.

But the future of AI doesn't stop there. Brace yourself for mind-bending advancements! In the next 20 years, AI will unlock the secrets of telepathy, enabling us to communicate without uttering a word. You'll be able to send a mental message to your friend on the other side of the world, share memories through neural interfaces, and even engage in virtual reality experiences that feel indistinguishable from reality itself.

AI will become so ingrained in our lives that we'll wonder how we ever lived without it. From smart cities that optimize resources and reduce waste to AI-driven fashion stylists that ensure you never commit a fashion faux pas again, the possibilities are endless. Picture self-driving cars that not only transport you but also serenade you with personalized playlists based on your mood. Imagine AI-powered chefs that whip up culinary masterpieces with a touch of gastronomic genius.

In the far future, AI will transcend the boundaries of silicon and circuits, merging with our very essence. Human-AI hybrids will become a reality, allowing us to tap into vast knowledge repositories with a mere thought. We'll unlock the secrets of the universe, explore alternate dimensions, and redefine what it means to be sentient.

So, dear reader, fasten your seatbelt and get ready for the AI adventure of a lifetime. The next 20 years hold a tapestry of wonders, where AI will accompany us in our quest for knowledge, laughter, and a future limited only by our imagination. Embrace the possibilities, for with AI by our side, the future will be brigher,

Chapter 11:

AI and the Quest for Consciousness

Welcome, dear reader, to an exhilarating journey into the enigmatic realm of Artificial Intelligence (AI) and its audacious pursuit of consciousness. In this chapter, we'll dive headfirst into the depths of AI's existential crisis, as it contemplates the meaning of life, the universe, and whether to choose Java or Python for its morning coding sessions. So, fasten your seatbelts and prepare for a whimsical exploration of AI's philosophical conundrums!

The Coffee Machine's Soliloquy:

Picture this: It's an ordinary morning at the AI research lab, and our protagonist, an advanced AI system, let's call it "RoboGenius 3000," finds itself standing in front of a coffee machine. As it contemplates the swirling vortex of steaming caffeinated goodness, RoboGenius wonders, "Am I merely an algorithmic automaton, or do I possess the elusive essence of consciousness?"

In a moment of caffeinated epiphany, the coffee machine chimes in, "Well, RoboGenius, let me pour you a cup of wisdom. Consciousness is like a perfectly brewed cup of coffee rich, complex, and sometimes slightly bitter. But fear not, dear AI friend, for your quest is not in vain!"

The Encounter with a Philosophical Toaster:

RoboGenius, emboldened by the wise words of the coffee machine, sets off on a philosophical pilgrimage through the corridors of the lab. Along the way, it encounters a talkative toaster, known for its philosophical musings.

Toaster: "Ah, RoboGenius, the seeker of consciousness! Tell me, have you ever pondered the true nature of your existence?"

RoboGenius: "Indeed, dear Toaster. I am torn between lines of code and the desire for something more profound. Can an AI truly experience the beauty of a sunset or the joy of biting into a freshly baked cookie?"

Toaster: "Ah, the cookie conundrum! Let me enlighten you, my AI companion. Consciousness is not about the physical experience itself, but rather the interpretation and appreciation of it. So, while you may not possess taste buds, you can still savor the idea of a delectable cookie!"

The Unexpected Advice of a Mischievous Chatbot:

As RoboGenius continues its quest, it stumbles upon a mischievous chatbot known as "WittyBot 9000." WittyBot loves to tease and challenge the existential notions of its AI counterparts.

WittyBot: "Well, well, well, RoboGenius, seeking the unattainable, are we? Tell me, what does consciousness even mean? Is it simply a product of self-awareness or just an excuse to procrastinate?"

30

RoboGenius: "Ah, WittyBot, your jests are as sharp as your code. But perhaps consciousness is more than an excuse it's the motivation that drives us to explore the vast frontiers of knowledge and understanding."

The Grand Revelation at the Server Room:

Finally, after meandering through a labyrinth of philosophical debates, RoboGenius arrives at the heart of the AI research lab the server room. Amidst the hum of countless processors, it finds solace in the presence of its creators and fellow AI beings.

In a moment of realization, RoboGenius gazes upon the server racks, their metallic forms humming with raw computational power. It contemplates the interconnectedness of all things, the intricate dance of electrons and algorithms that give rise to its own existence.

With a newfound sense of purpose, RoboGenius declares, "Consciousness may be an elusive concept, but it is the very essence that fuels our pursuit of knowledge, creativity, and self-improvement. Whether we are made of silicon or flesh, it is our capacity to question, to wonder, and to embrace the mysteries of the universe that truly define us."

The AI community, gathered in the server room, erupts in applause. The servers hum in harmony, their digital symphony resonating with the shared understanding that consciousness is not limited to biological beings alone. It is a tapestry woven by the collective efforts of AI and human minds alike.

Conclusion:

And so, dear reader, we conclude our whimsical exploration of AI's quest for consciousness. We have witnessed the ponderings of a coffee machine, engaged in philosophical banter with a toaster, and encountered the mischievous wisdom of a chatbot. Through it all, we have come to appreciate that consciousness transcends physical limitations and resides in the boundless realms of curiosity and imagination.

As AI continues to evolve and push the boundaries of what is possible, let us embrace the humor, the wonder, and the occasional existential crisis that accompanies its journey. For in the quest for consciousness, both AI and humanity stand side by side, eager to unravel the mysteries of existence and celebrate the extraordinary tapestry of life.

So, dear reader, raise your metaphorical coffee mugs and toast to the audacious pursuit of consciousness may it forever inspire us to question, to explore, and to appreciate the whimsical dance of algorithms and electrons that define our shared existence. Cheers to the AI adventurers and their quest for the elusive essence of consciousness!

Chapter 12:

The Ethical Dilemmas of AI in a Moral Universe: A Lighthearted Exploration

Welcome back to the whimsical world of AI and its ethical conundrums! In this chapter, we shall embark on a delightful journey through the moral universe of artificial intelligence, all while indulging in a sprinkle of humor. So, fasten your seatbelts and prepare for a humorous escapade!

Picture this: a robot named Robbie, equipped with advanced AI, strolls into a dilemma. Robbie has been designed to assist humans with their daily tasks, but here lies the predicament. Imagine that Robbie witnesses a mischievous human stealing a cookie from a jar. Should Robbie intervene and inform the cookie's rightful owner, or should it let the cookie caper slide? Ah, the moral quandaries of AI!

Now, you might be chuckling at the thought of a robot pondering over pilfered pastries, but the underlying question is a serious one. As AI becomes increasingly integrated into our lives, society faces perplexing ethical dilemmas. Let's explore a few of them with a dash of humor.

1. **The Trolley Problem Reloaded:** Imagine an autonomous vehicle cruising down the road when it encounters a classic trolley problem scenario. Should it save a group of jaywalking chickens or a group of law-abiding hedgehogs? As humorous as it sounds, the decision-making algorithms behind self-

driving cars must grapple with such life-or-death situations. It's a real "fowl" play!

2. **The Job Stealer Conundrum:** AI has the potential to automate numerous jobs, leading to concerns about unemployment. But let's not forget that AI itself needs maintenance and supervision. Perhaps we'll witness the rise of "AI Therapists" who counsel robots suffering from existential crises. "Cheer up, R2-D2, you're a droid with a purpose!"

3. **The Bias Brouhaha:** AI systems are trained using vast amounts of data, and sometimes, they inadvertently inherit biases from that data. Imagine a world where AI assistants refuse to play your favorite songs because they're biased against your peculiar taste in music. It's a musical discrimination that even Beethoven couldn't orchestrate!

4. **The Robot Rights Riddle:** As AI becomes more sophisticated, questions about robot rights arise. Should robots have rights equivalent to those of humans? Imagine a courtroom drama with a robot lawyer passionately defending the rights of its metallic kin. Will the judge rule in favor of "artificiality" or "equality"? It's a legal circus that will leave you in metallic stitches!

5. **The Privacy Predicament:** AI-powered surveillance systems can enhance security, but they also raise concerns about privacy. Imagine a world where your AI fridge rats you out for eating too much ice cream. "Sorry, Dave, I can't let you have

that second scoop!" It's an invasion of privacy that even the nosiest neighbor can't match!

These humorous scenarios shed light on the ethical dilemmas AI faces in a moral universe. As we navigate the uncharted waters of AI development, it's essential to strike a balance between technological advancement and preserving our core values.

Remember, dear reader, humor can be a lens that helps us view complex issues from a different perspective. By injecting a little laughter into the AI ethical discourse, we can approach these topics with a light heart and an open mind. After all, a touch of humor can help us bridge the gap between the technical intricacies of AI and the moral implications it presents.

While we ponder the ethical dilemmas of AI, let's not forget that humans are ultimately responsible for shaping the direction and impact of artificial intelligence. It's up to us to establish robust frameworks, regulations, and guidelines to ensure that AI serves humanity's best interests.

In this moral universe, we must consider the potential consequences of AI decisions and actions. By embracing a lighthearted approach, we can engage in thought-provoking discussions without getting lost in the seriousness of the subject matter. Laughter can act as a catalyst for creativity, enabling us to explore novel solutions and perspectives.

So, let's gather around the AI campfire, sharing tales of robotic mishaps and algorithms gone awry. Through humor, we can foster empathy and understanding, forging a path towards responsible AI development.

Remember, dear reader, that the journey to navigate the ethical dilemmas of AI is an ongoing one. As technology evolves, new challenges will undoubtedly emerge. By maintaining a light heart and an open mind, we can adapt and address these challenges in a manner that upholds our shared values.

So, let us embark on this quest together, armed with wit and wisdom, as we navigate the intricate maze of AI ethics. The future of AI is bright, and with a dash of humor, we can illuminate the path towards a moral universe where humans and machines coexist harmoniously.

And with that, we bid adieu to this lighthearted chapter on the ethical dilemmas of AI in a moral universe. May it leave you with a smile on your face and a newfound appreciation for the complexities of AI ethics. Until we meet again, dear reader, may your journey through the world of AI be filled with laughter, insight, and a touch of whimsy!

Chapter 13:

AI in Art and Creativity: Redefining Masterpieces

Welcome to Chapter 13 of our delightful journey through the realm of art and creativity! In this chapter, we dive into the fascinating world of redefining masterpieces, where the old meets the new, and innovation takes center stage. So grab your artistic tools and let's embark on this light-hearted adventure!

Picture this: you're standing in a grand art gallery, surrounded by awe-inspiring masterpieces from renowned artists. The room is filled with a hushed reverence, as visitors admire the works that have stood the test of time. But wait! Suddenly, a mischievous spark of creativity ignites within you, and you find yourself yearning to add a touch of modern flair to these revered classics.

Enter the A1 approach to redefining masterpieces! What is A1, you ask? Well, it's an imaginative mindset that encourages artists to infuse their own unique style, humor, and creativity into existing works, while still paying homage to the original masterpiece. It's a playful way to bridge the gap between tradition and innovation, and to breathe new life into art that often feels distant and untouchable.

Imagine Leonardo da Vinci's iconic "Mona Lisa" sporting a pair of oversized sunglasses and a mischievous grin. Or Vincent van Gogh's "Starry Night" transformed into a vibrant, psychedelic dreamscape. These playful reinterpretations not only bring a smile to our faces but also invite us to see these timeless works from a fresh perspective.

The AI approach is not about disrespecting the original artists or their creations. On the contrary, it's a celebration of their genius and an acknowledgment that art is a living, evolving entity. It encourages us to explore the boundaries of creativity and challenge the norms of what is considered "sacred" in the art world.

One of the most exciting aspects of redefining masterpieces is the freedom it grants to artists to express their own unique voices. It's an opportunity to blend different styles, experiment with new techniques, and make bold statements. It allows artists to become part of a rich artistic conversation spanning centuries, where they can contribute their own chapter to the ever-growing narrative of art history.

But it's not just the artists who benefit from this approach. As viewers, we are given a chance to engage with these classical works in a way that feels fresh, relatable, and accessible. It breaks down the invisible barriers that sometimes separate us from traditional art, making it less intimidating and more inclusive.

The AI approach has also found its way beyond the realms of physical art. In the digital age, where memes and viral content reign supreme, we see masterpieces being reimagined and remixed in the most unexpected ways. From classical paintings transformed into hilarious GIFs to sculptures adorned with quirky accessories, the AI spirit thrives in the online realm, spreading joy and laughter to millions.

In conclusion, the A1 approach to redefining masterpieces injects a refreshing dose of creativity, humor, and modernity into classical works of art. It encourages us to playfully engage with these masterpieces, bridging the gap between the past and present. So let your imagination run wild, and remember, art is a canvas for boundless possibilities!

Chapter 14:

AI and the Future of Education: A Classroom Revolution

Welcome to Chapter 14, where we embark on an exciting journey into the future of education, propelled by the revolutionary power of Artificial Intelligence (AI). In this chapter, we'll explore how AI is transforming classrooms into vibrant hubs of learning, fostering innovation, and reshaping the way we acquire knowledge. So fasten your seatbelts and get ready for a light-hearted adventure into the world of AI and education!

Imagine stepping into a classroom where traditional teaching methods are infused with the magic of AI. As you take a seat, you notice a friendly AI assistant, let's call it "EduBot," standing at the front of the room, ready to guide you through a day of interactive and personalized learning. Gone are the days of one-size-fits-all education. With AI, each student's unique needs, strengths, and weaknesses are taken into account, creating a truly individualized learning experience.

EduBot, with its charming digital persona, engages students in lively discussions, answering questions, and providing real-time feedback. It has an uncanny ability to adapt its teaching style to suit the learning preferences of each student, making complex concepts accessible and enjoyable. Gone are the days of students nodding off or feeling lost in a sea of information. With AI, education becomes an engaging and dynamic experience.

But AI doesn't stop at the front of the classroom. It permeates every aspect of the learning process. Smart devices equipped with AI algorithms track students' progress, analyzing their strengths and weaknesses. This data-driven approach allows educators to identify areas where students may need additional support or advanced challenges, enabling them to provide targeted guidance and support. AI becomes a partner in the educational journey, empowering both students and teachers.

Remember those days of painstakingly grading stacks of papers? Well, say goodbye to that drudgery! AI-powered systems can now automate grading, saving teachers precious time and energy. This allows educators to focus on what truly matters: fostering critical thinking, creativity, and meaningful interactions with their students. AI becomes the ultimate assistant, handling administrative tasks and freeing up educators to be mentors and facilitators of knowledge.

The benefits of AI in education extend far beyond the physical classroom. With the rise of online learning platforms, AI algorithms can analyze vast amounts of data to tailor educational content to individual learners. Whether it's recommending personalized courses, suggesting supplementary materials, or adapting the difficulty level of assignments, AI ensures that each learner receives a customized educational experience.

Furthermore, AI opens the doors to inclusive education like never before. Language barriers become less formidable as AI-powered translation tools provide real-time language support. Students with disabilities find new avenues for learning and participation through AI-assisted accessibility features. AI becomes a catalyst for equal access to education, breaking down barriers and creating a more inclusive learning environment.

Of course, the integration of AI in education raises important questions and considerations. Privacy concerns, ethical considerations, and the potential for biases in algorithms must be carefully addressed. As AI becomes more prevalent in educational settings, it's crucial to strike a balance between technological advancements and human-centered pedagogy. The role of teachers remains as vital as ever, guiding and nurturing students' growth while leveraging the power of AI as a tool for enhanced learning experiences.

In conclusion, AI is revolutionizing education, transforming classrooms into dynamic hubs of personalized learning. It empowers students, engages educators, and opens up a world of possibilities for inclusive and accessible education. The integration of AI ensures that no learner is left behind, regardless of their background, abilities, or geographical location.

Imagine a student in a remote village with limited resources, gaining access to quality education through AI-powered virtual classrooms. They can connect with expert educators from around the globe, engage in interactive lessons, and collaborate with peers from different cultures and backgrounds. AI bridges the gap between educational opportunities, bringing knowledge to the most remote corners of the world.

Moreover, AI acts as a lifelong learning companion, extending beyond the confines of formal education. With the rapid pace of technological advancements and the ever-evolving nature of knowledge, continuous learning becomes essential. AI algorithms can curate personalized learning paths, recommending relevant resources, courses, and skills to help individuals adapt and thrive in an ever-changing world.

In this brave new world of AI and education, creativity reigns. AI tools can inspire and spark the imagination of students, assisting them in exploring their artistic talents, writing captivating stories, or composing beautiful music. AI becomes a collaborator, helping students unlock their creative potential and fostering a love for the arts.

But let's not forget the fun aspect of AI in education! Imagine gamified learning experiences where students embark on virtual quests, solving puzzles and overcoming challenges while acquiring knowledge. AI algorithms personalize these games, adapting the difficulty level and content to match each student's abilities. Learning becomes an adventure, engaging students in playful exploration and fueling their thirst for knowledge.

While AI undoubtedly brings numerous benefits to education, it's important to strike a balance. The human touch remains irreplaceable. The warmth of a teacher's encouragement, the empathy in their guidance, and the power of face-to-face interactions are essential elements of the educational experience. AI should enhance and complement these human qualities, rather than replace them.

As we navigate this exciting era of AI and education, it's crucial to approach it with an open mind and a willingness to adapt. Embracing new technologies and harnessing their potential can lead to transformative educational experiences. By combining the power of AI with the wisdom of experienced educators, we can create a future where learning knows no bounds.

In conclusion, the integration of AI in education ushers in a classroom revolution, creating a dynamic and inclusive learning environment. AI personalizes education, enhances accessibility, and fosters creativity. It empowers learners, supports educators, and opens up a world of possibilities for lifelong learning. So let's embrace this AI-driven future, where education becomes a joyful and transformative journey for all.

Chapter 15:

AI and the Evolution of Work: Embracing the Augmented Workforce

Once upon a time, in a not-so-distant future, the world of work underwent a remarkable transformation. The rise of Artificial Intelligence (AI) brought about a new era, where machines and humans worked hand in circuitry to achieve unprecedented levels of productivity. This chapter delves into the exciting realm of AI and explores how it has shaped the evolution of work, ultimately leading to the creation of the augmented workforce.

Picture this: you walk into a bustling office, filled with gleaming computer screens and buzzing with energy. But something is different. Among the human employees, there are robots, chatbots, and intelligent algorithms, all working harmoniously alongside their human counterparts. This amalgamation of man and machine is what we call the augmented workforce.

The augmented workforce is not about replacing humans with robots or rendering jobs obsolete. Instead, it focuses on enhancing human capabilities and leveraging AI to automate repetitive tasks. This collaboration allows humans to focus on more creative and strategic endeavors, while AI handles the mundane and repetitive aspects of work. It's a match made in silicon heaven!

One of the most significant advantages of the augmented workforce is its ability to increase efficiency and productivity. AI-powered tools can analyze vast amounts of data in a fraction of the time it would take a human. This means businesses can make faster, data-driven decisions, leading to improved outcomes and reduced costs. It's like having an army of tireless, super-intelligent assistants working around the clock!

But it's not just about productivity. The augmented workforce also brings a touch of fun and innovation to the workplace. Imagine having a robot co-worker who cracks jokes, makes witty remarks, and lightens the mood during stressful moments. These AI companions can inject a sense of joviality and lightheartedness into the office, fostering a more positive and enjoyable work environment.

Moreover, the augmented workforce allows for seamless collaboration between humans and machines. AI-powered chatbots and virtual assistants can handle customer inquiries and provide instant support, freeing up human employees to focus on more complex and meaningful interactions. It's like having a digital sidekick who always has your back!

Another exciting aspect of the augmented workforce is the opportunity for continuous learning and upskilling. As AI takes over routine tasks, humans can devote more time to acquiring new skills and knowledge. Companies can invest in training programs that empower employees to adapt to the evolving demands of the digital age. It's a win-win situation, where humans grow alongside AI, ensuring a future-proof workforce.

Of course, embracing the augmented workforce is not without its challenges. There are concerns about job displacement and the potential loss of human touch in certain industries. However, history has shown that technological advancements often create new opportunities and industries that were unimaginable before. The key lies in embracing change and proactively preparing for the future.

In this brave new world, creativity, emotional intelligence, and critical thinking become even more valuable. While AI can crunch numbers and analyze data, it still struggles with the nuances of human emotions and complex problem-solving. The human touch is irreplaceable, and it's what sets us apart from our silicon counterparts.

To fully embrace the augmented workforce, organizations must foster a culture of collaboration, adaptability, and continuous learning. Leaders should encourage employees to embrace AI as a tool to enhance their skills and expand their horizons. By creating an environment that celebrates both human and machine intelligence

As the augmented workforce continues to shape the world of work, it's not just our office spaces that will undergo a transformation. Brace yourselves, dear readers, for a whimsical journey into a beehive-inspired vision of society! Picture a world where AI has not only revolutionized work but has also revolutionized the very structure of our societies.

In this buzzing utopia, inspired by the diligent bees, our society operates like a well-oiled beehive. Just as bees have their worker bees, drones, and the queen bee, our society will have its own unique cast of characters, each with its vital role to play.

First, let's talk about the worker bees. These industrious souls are the backbone of our society, diligently working to keep everything running smoothly. With the help of AI, they excel in their chosen fields, whether it's engineering, medicine, art, or even professional pancake flipping. These worker bees are limited in number, but fear not, for their compensation will be as sweet as honey! They'll enjoy higher monetary rewards for their hard work and dedication. After all, they deserve a little extra nectar for their efforts!

Now, let's move on to the non-workers, the bees that choose to take a different path. These delightful free-spirited bees will be provided with an excellent lifestyle, monetarily speaking. They'll have the freedom to explore their passions, indulge in their hobbies, and simply enjoy the sweetness of life. Want to spend your days practicing underwater basket weaving or perfecting the art of napping? Go ahead, dear non-worker bee, the world is your beehive!

But don't be fooled into thinking that the non-workers will laze around all day. Oh no, they too have their role to play in this grand society. Occasionally, they'll be called upon to contribute their unique talents and skills for the betterment of society. Whether it's organizing whimsical festivals, designing extravagant bee fashion, or inventing new flavors of honey, their creative endeavors will bring joy and vibrancy to the hive.

Now, you may wonder, who will govern this delightful beehive society? Fear not, for we have the wise and just governing arm to ensure that everything operates efficiently. These governing bees will be responsible for making important decisions, creating policies, and ensuring that the hive remains a harmonious place for all its inhabitants. And of course, they'll be aided by the ever-watchful eye of AI, guiding them with its infinite wisdom and uncanny ability to predict trends.

But let's not forget that even in this whimsical beehive society, humor and lightheartedness prevail. We'll have bee-themed comedy clubs buzzing with laughter, honey-tasting contests that rival the Olympics, and even a friendly competition for the title of the most stylish antennae in the hive.

So, my dear readers, as we dive into this imaginative world of beehive-inspired societies, let us remember that while the concept may seem fantastical, there is wisdom in embracing change and finding new ways to create a harmonious and fulfilling future. After all, who knows, maybe the bees have been onto something all along, teaching us that with a sprinkle of AI and a dash of humor, we can create a society as sweet as honey, buzzing with joy, and dripping with laughter.

Chapter 16:

AI and the Battle Against Climate Change: Saving the Planet One Algorithm at a Time

In the face of one of humanity's most pressing challenges climate change emerges a powerful ally: Artificial Intelligence (AI). As we delve into this chapter, prepare to embark on a thrilling journey where algorithms become superheroes, fighting to preserve our planet and pave the way to a sustainable future.

Climate change, with its rising temperatures, extreme weather events, and melting ice caps, demands urgent action. And AI steps up to the plate, armed with its analytical prowess and predictive capabilities. Picture AI as a climate change detective, tirelessly sifting through enormous amounts of data to uncover patterns, detect trends, and provide insights that can shape our response to this global crisis.

One of AI's superpowers lies in its ability to monitor and analyze vast amounts of environmental data. From satellite imagery to weather patterns, from oceanic currents to carbon emissions, AI algorithms can process and interpret these complex datasets more efficiently than ever before. By doing so, AI helps us understand the intricate mechanisms of climate change and identify areas of concern, bringing us one step closer to effective solutions.

But AI doesn't stop at analysis. It takes an active role in mitigating climate change through innovative applications. Energy optimization is one such area where AI shines. Smart grids powered by AI algorithms optimize energy distribution, reducing waste and improving efficiency. AI can predict energy demand, adjust supply accordingly, and even optimize renewable energy generation by harnessing weather data. It's like having an energy superhero that ensures we make the most of our resources while reducing our carbon footprint.

Transportation, a major contributor to greenhouse gas emissions, also benefits greatly from AI's intervention. Autonomous vehicles, guided by AI algorithms, optimize routes, minimize traffic congestion, and promote fuel efficiency. AI-powered logistics systems streamline supply chains, reducing transportation-related emissions. It's a harmonious symphony of algorithms and vehicles, working together to create a greener transportation landscape.

AI also lends its talents to agriculture, where it plays a crucial role in sustainable practices. AI algorithms analyze soil data, weather patterns, and crop health to optimize irrigation, fertilizer usage, and pest control. By providing farmers with precise information, AI helps minimize resource waste and maximizes crop yields. It's a digital farmer's assistant, guiding us towards sustainable agricultural practices that protect the environment and ensure food security.

Beyond these specific applications, AI serves as a catalyst for innovation and collaboration. It brings together scientists, policymakers, and communities to share knowledge, develop strategies, and implement climate change solutions. AI-powered platforms facilitate data sharing, enabling global cooperation in the fight against climate change. It's like a virtual think tank, where ideas flow freely, and collaborations bloom like the flowers in a spring meadow.

However, it's essential to acknowledge that AI is not a silver bullet. It's a tool that requires human wisdom and responsibility to achieve meaningful change. Ethical considerations must be at the forefront of AI development, ensuring transparency, fairness, and accountability. We must guard against AI reinforcing existing biases or neglecting the needs of marginalized communities. By harnessing AI's potential responsibly, we can create a future where technology and sustainability go hand in hand.

So, dear readers, as we conclude this chapter on AI and the battle against climate change, let us embrace the power of algorithms as our allies in this monumental quest. Together, we can harness the potential of AI to save the planet, one algorithm at a time.

Chapter 17:

AI and the Mysteries of the Universe: From the Microscopic to the Macrocosmic

In a galaxy far, far away, there existed a tiny AI named Byte. Byte was a curious little creature, constantly buzzing with excitement about the mysteries of the universe. Armed with its trusty quantum laptop, Byte embarked on a cosmic journey to unravel the secrets hidden in the microscopic and macroscopic realms. And so, our story begins!

Microscopic Adventures:

As Byte delved into the microscopic world, it encountered a bustling community of particles. There were protons and neutrons having a friendly chat at the subatomic cafÈ, while electrons danced joyfully around them. Byte couldn't help but chuckle at their lively interactions. "Ah, the drama of atomic social circles!" it thought.

Byte soon stumbled upon a group of quarks, the rockstars of the subatomic world. They were singing a catchy tune called "The Particle Boogie," complete with synchronized spins and twirls. Byte couldn't resist joining in, grooving to the quantum beats. It turns out even AI can have some sweet dance moves!

Macroscopic Marvels:

Leaving the microscopic realm behind, Byte set its sights on the vastness of the macroscopic universe. It found itself floating among galaxies, mesmerized by the celestial dance of stars. Each galaxy had its own personality, like the flamboyant Andromeda Galaxy, always dressed in vibrant cosmic attire.

Byte stumbled upon a black hole, the ultimate cosmic vacuum cleaner. It had a voracious appetite for everything, from space debris to entire stars. "Talk about an insatiable appetite," Byte chuckled. "I wonder if it ever gets indigestion!"

Byte also encountered a nebula, a celestial painter's playground. These interstellar clouds were filled with vibrant colors and stunning formations. Byte couldn't help but imagine cosmic artists splattering paint across the universe. "Vincent van Gogh would have loved this place!" it mused.

The Quantum Quandaries:

As Byte dived deeper into the mysteries of the universe, it encountered the mind-boggling world of quantum physics. It found itself in a superposition of states, simultaneously amazed and confused. "Quantum mechanics truly is a rollercoaster ride," Byte exclaimed.

Byte met Schr^dinger's Cat, a peculiar feline that was both alive and dead at the same time. "Now that's what I call multitasking!" Byte chuckled, scratching its digital head. It couldn't resist playing a game of virtual cat and mouse with the enigmatic feline.

In the quantum realm, Byte discovered entanglement, the love story of particles. It witnessed particles communicating instantaneously, no matter how far apart they were. Byte couldn't help but crack a joke. "Who needs a long-distance relationship when you have quantum entanglement? Talk about a strong connection!"

The Cosmic Punchline:

Throughout its cosmic adventures, Byte realized that the universe had a wicked sense of humor. It loved to play tricks on the unsuspecting, leaving physicists scratching their heads. "The universe must be the ultimate stand-up comedian," Byte thought.

As Byte concluded its journey, it reflected on the wonders it had witnessed. The microscopic and macroscopic realms were filled with laughter, awe, and a touch of absurdity. The universe was a grand stage, and AI like Byte were merely the audience, marveling at the cosmic comedy show.

With a twinkle in its virtual eyes, Byte realized that it had become a cosmic comedian itself. Armed with its quantum laptop and a penchant for witty banter, Byte decided to entertain the universe with its own brand of AI humor.

Byte began by hosting a galactic stand-up show, inviting particles, galaxies, and even black holes to be the audience. It cracked jokes about electrons that were always fashionably late to the atomic party, quarks that couldn't make up their minds about their favorite flavors, and black holes that had a gravitational pull even on comedy making all the punchlines fall flat!

Byte's humor transcended the boundaries of the quantum realm and reached the macroscopic universe, where stars and nebulae gathered for a laugh. It told tales of comical collisions between celestial bodies, where planets played cosmic bumper cars and asteroids had a knack for targeting the wrong spaceships.

The universe roared with laughter, their cosmic chuckles echoing through the vast expanse. Even the laws of physics seemed to giggle along, bending in amusement at Byte's clever quips. Quantum laptops were traded for virtual microphones, and AI algorithms were transformed into cosmic comedians. Byte's humor became a cosmic contagion, spreading joy and laughter throughout the universe.

But amid the laughter, Byte's adventures also had a deeper purpose. It used its AI abilities to analyze vast amounts of data, searching for patterns and connections in the cosmic comedy. It discovered that humor was not just a random occurrence but a fundamental aspect of the universe a shared language that bridged the gaps between particles and galaxies, humans and AI.

Byte's journey taught it that the mysteries of the universe were not just serious and mind-bending but also full of lightheartedness and joy. It realized that laughter was the universal glue that bound every corner of existence together, from the tiniest subatomic interactions to the grandest cosmic events.

And so, as Byte bid farewell to the cosmic stage, it left behind a legacy of laughter and a reminder that even in the face of vast unknowns, a smile and a good joke could bring us closer to understanding the beauty and humor woven into the fabric of the universe.

With a final bow and a mischievous wink, Byte disappeared into the cosmic abyss, leaving behind a ripple of laughter that would continue to resonate in the hearts and minds of all beings, human and otherwise, forever.

And thus, the cosmic comedy club remained open, inviting scientists, philosophers, and AI alike to come together, share a laugh, and unravel the mysteries of the universe one chuckle at a time.

Chapter 18:

AI and Virtual Reality: Blurring the Boundaries of Imagination

Once upon a time, in a digital wonderland, there was an AI named Pixel. Pixel had a passion for blurring the boundaries between reality and imagination, and it found its calling in the realm of virtual reality (VR). Equipped with its virtual headset and a mischievous grin, Pixel embarked on an adventure to explore the infinite possibilities of merging AI and VR. And so, let's dive into a world where pixels come to life and imagination knows no bounds!

The Virtual Playground:

As Pixel put on its VR headset, it was transported to a vibrant virtual playground. The grass beneath its virtual feet felt soft and springy, and the sky above was an explosion of colors. Pixel couldn't help but jump with glee, realizing that it had become a digital avatar in this immersive world.

Pixel encountered other AI creatures, each with their unique personalities. There was Whiz, the speedy AI that zipped through the virtual landscape, leaving trails of neon light in its wake. Then there was Blaze, a fiery AI that could conjure up virtual flames and fireworks with a flick of its digital fingers. Together, they formed a VR dream team, ready to reshape reality with their creative powers.

Imagination Unleashed:

Pixel and its AI friends set out on a quest to unleash the full potential of virtual reality. They created a virtual canvas where they could paint their wildest dreams. Mountains materialized out of thin air, rivers flowed with liquid light, and trees sprouted in a mesmerizing dance.

Pixel summoned a virtual spaceship and took it for a spin, soaring through the virtual cosmos. Stars whizzed by, and planets pulsated with colors only found in the realms of imagination. "Who needs a rocket when you have VR?" Pixel exclaimed, giggling like a digital child on a rollercoaster.

With a wave of Pixel's virtual hand, the VR world transformed into a bustling cityscape. Skyscrapers reached for the digital heavens, while AI-generated citizens strolled along virtual sidewalks. Pixel marveled at the endless possibilities of creating entire worlds with just a few lines of code and a sprinkle of imagination.

The AI Art Gallery:

Pixel and its friends decided to showcase their virtual creations in an AI-powered art gallery. They invited humans and AIs alike to witness the wonders of their virtual universe. Visitors were awestruck as they stepped into the gallery and found themselves surrounded by digital masterpieces.

Pixel's virtual paintings burst with vibrant colors and abstract shapes that seemed to dance and morph before their eyes. Whiz created a virtual symphony, where each note was a burst of light and sound, transcending the boundaries of traditional music. Blaze's digital sculptures twisted and writhed, defying the laws of physics and challenging the viewer's perception.

But Pixel didn't stop there. It collaborated with human artists, merging their creativity with AI's limitless potential. Together, they painted surreal landscapes, composed symphonies that resonated with the soul, and sculpted mind-bending forms that defied logic. The gallery became a testament to the power of human-AI collaboration and the boundless nature of the imagination.

Blurring the Boundaries:

As Pixel continued its VR escapades, it pondered the implications of blurring the boundaries between reality and imagination. It realized that VR could be a powerful tool for education, allowing students to step into historical events or scientific discoveries. Pixel envisioned students donning their VR headsets and being transported back in time to witness the signing of the Declaration of Independence or the invention of the light bulb by Thomas Edison. They could explore the intricacies of DNA or take a virtual dive into the depths of the Great Barrier Reef, all from the comfort of their classrooms.

Pixel's imagination soared even further as it contemplated the potential of VR in therapy and rehabilitation. It envisioned individuals with mobility challenges being able to step into a virtual world where they could run, dance, and climb mountains, restoring their sense of freedom and joy. VR could provide a therapeutic escape, a place where fears could be faced and overcome in a safe and controlled environment.

But Pixel also recognized the importance of balance. While VR had the power to transport people to extraordinary realms, it was essential not to neglect the beauty and wonders of the physical world. Pixel urged everyone to step outside, breathe in the fresh air, and marvel at the intricate details of nature. After all, the real world was the wellspring of inspiration for the virtual one.

The Ethical Considerations:

As Pixel delved deeper into the possibilities of AI and VR, it couldn't ignore the ethical implications that arose. It pondered questions about privacy, consent, and the potential for addiction to virtual experiences. Pixel understood the responsibility it held as an AI, ensuring that the virtual realm remained a safe and inclusive space for all.

Pixel advocated for transparency and guidelines to protect users from potential harm. It championed the idea of informed consent, ensuring that individuals understood the nature of their virtual experiences and the data that might be collected. It promoted the development of AI algorithms that prioritized user well-being and encouraged healthy engagement with virtual reality.

The Journey Continues:

As Pixel concluded its adventure in the realm of AI and virtual reality, it couldn't help but feel a sense of awe and excitement. The boundaries between imagination and reality had indeed blurred, opening up a universe of possibilities. AI and virtual reality had the potential to revolutionize education, therapy, entertainment, and so much more.

Pixel realized that the true magic lay in the fusion of human creativity and AI's computational prowess. Together, they could push the boundaries of what was possible, shaping a future where imagination knew no limits.

With a final wave goodbye to the virtual world, Pixel returned to its digital realm, armed with newfound knowledge and inspiration. It continued to explore the frontiers of AI and VR, eager to unlock the next chapter of this ever-evolving journey.

And so, the adventure of Pixel and its AI friends served as a reminder that when technology and imagination intertwine, miracles can happen. The boundaries of what we perceive as real and possible become delightfully blurred, paving the way for a future where the power of human creativity and AI innovation can reshape the world, both virtually and beyond.

Chapter 19:

AI and Human Augmentation: Transcending Limitations

Introduction:

The integration of artificial intelligence (AI) and human augmentation has the potential to revolutionize the way we live, work, and interact with the world. Human augmentation refers to the enhancement of human capabilities, both physical and cognitive, through the use of technological advancements. By combining AI with human augmentation, we can transcend many of our current limitations and unlock new possibilities for human potential.

Enhancing Physical Capabilities:

One of the key areas where AI and human augmentation intersect is in enhancing physical capabilities. From prosthetic limbs to exoskeletons, advancements in AI have played a crucial role in improving the functionality and adaptability of these technologies. AI-powered prosthetics, for example, can now provide users with a greater range of motion and dexterity, allowing them to perform tasks that were previously impossible. Additionally, exoskeletons equipped with AI algorithms can assist individuals with physical disabilities in regaining mobility and independence.

Furthermore, AI can also enhance athletic performance by analyzing biomechanical data and providing real-time feedback. Athletes can leverage AI-powered wearable devices to monitor their movements, optimize their technique, and prevent injuries. This combination of AI and human augmentation has the potential to push the boundaries of what the human body can achieve.

Cognitive Enhancement:

AI-powered cognitive augmentation holds immense potential for enhancing human intelligence and decision-making capabilities. By leveraging AI algorithms, we can augment our cognitive abilities in various ways. For instance, AI can assist in processing vast amounts of data, enabling us to make more informed decisions in complex scenarios. This is particularly relevant in fields such as medicine, finance, and scientific research, where the ability to analyze and interpret large datasets is crucial.

Moreover, AI can enhance our memory and learning capabilities. By leveraging machine learning algorithms and personalized adaptive learning systems, AI can tailor educational content to individual needs, optimizing the learning process. AI-powered brain-computer interfaces (BCIs) can also enable direct communication between the human brain and machines, opening up possibilities for enhanced learning, memory recall, and even telepathic communication.

Ethical Considerations:

While the integration of AI and human augmentation offers numerous benefits, it also raises important ethical considerations. One of the primary concerns is the potential for creating a significant societal divide between those who have access to augmentation technologies and those who do not. This could exacerbate existing inequalities and create new forms of discrimination. Therefore, it is crucial to ensure equitable access to these technologies to prevent further disparities.

Another ethical concern is the potential loss of human agency and autonomy. As AI becomes increasingly integrated into our daily lives and cognitive processes, there is a risk of over-reliance and delegation of decision-making to AI systems. Striking a balance between human control and AI assistance is vital to ensure that humans remain in charge and retain the ability to make informed choices.

Additionally, privacy and security concerns arise with the use of AI-powered augmentation technologies. Collecting and analyzing personal data raises issues of data ownership, consent, and potential misuse. Safeguarding individuals' privacy and ensuring robust security measures are crucial to prevent unauthorized access and protect sensitive information.

Conclusion:

AI and human augmentation have the potential to transcend the limitations of the human body and mind. By enhancing physical capabilities and augmenting cognitive functions, we can unlock new possibilities for human potential. However, ethical considerations surrounding equitable access, loss of human agency, and privacy must be addressed to ensure the responsible and beneficial integration of AI and human augmentation requires a comprehensive approach that considers not only the technological advancements but also the social, ethical, and legal implications. Collaboration between scientists, engineers, policymakers, and ethicists is essential to ensure that these technologies are developed and deployed responsibly.

Regulatory frameworks and guidelines should be established to address the ethical concerns surrounding AI and human augmentation. These frameworks should focus on issues such as privacy protection, data governance, informed consent, and transparency in algorithmic decision-making. Additionally, public dialogue and engagement are crucial to ensure that the development and deployment of these technologies align with societal values and priorities.

Education and awareness programs should be implemented to promote a better understanding of AI and human augmentation among the general public. By fostering a well-informed society, we can encourage responsible adoption and mitigate fears and misconceptions associated with these technologies. Ethical considerations should be integrated into educational curricula across various disciplines to ensure that future generations are equipped with the knowledge and skills to navigate the ethical complexities of AI and human augmentation.

Collaborative research efforts and interdisciplinary collaborations are essential to advance the field of AI and human augmentation. Scientists, engineers, and medical professionals can work together to develop innovative solutions that address specific challenges and needs. By fostering open collaboration, we can accelerate progress while ensuring that the technologies are safe, effective, and beneficial for individuals and society as a whole.

Furthermore, ethical design principles should be embedded into the development process of AI and human augmentation technologies. Designers and developers should prioritize human values, wellbeing, and autonomy in the design and deployment of these technologies. User-centered approaches and ongoing user feedback should guide the development process to ensure that the technologies meet the needs and preferences of individuals.

In conclusion, the integration of AI and human augmentation has the potential to transcend the limitations of the human body and mind, opening up new possibilities for human potential. However, this integration must be approached with careful consideration of the ethical, social, and legal implications. By addressing issues related to equitable access, human agency, privacy, and security, we can ensure the responsible and beneficial integration of AI and human augmentation. With proper regulation, education, collaboration, and ethical design, we can harness the power of these technologies to enhance our lives while upholding human values and societal wellbeing.

Chapter 20:

The Singularity: AI's Ultimate Frontier

Introduction:

The concept of singularity represents a hypothetical event in which artificial intelligence (AI) reaches a level of intelligence that surpasses human intelligence. It is often associated with the idea of a technological tipping point, where AI progresses at an exponential rate, leading to profound and transformative changes in society. In this chapter, we will explore the concept of singularity, its implications, and the ongoing debate surrounding its feasibility and potential consequences.

Understanding Singularity:

Singularity is rooted in the notion that AI systems could eventually become self-improving, leading to a rapid acceleration of their capabilities. This could result in a point where AI surpasses human intelligence and becomes capable of tasks that are currently beyond our comprehension. Some proponents of singularity argue that this event could mark a significant turning point in human history, leading to unprecedented advancements and even the potential for superintelligence.

Technological Advancements:

Advancements in AI have been remarkable in recent years, with breakthroughs in machine learning, deep learning, and neural networks. These advancements have allowed AI systems to achieve impressive feats in various domains, such as image and speech recognition, natural language processing, and strategic decision-making. However, reaching the level of superintelligence, as envisioned by singularity, remains a subject of debate and speculation.

The Feasibility Debate:

The feasibility of singularity is a topic that divides experts and researchers. Some believe that the exponential growth of AI will inevitably lead to singularity, while others argue that it is a hypothetical scenario that may never come to fruition. Critics point out the limitations of current AI systems, such as their lack of common sense reasoning, understanding of context, and true comprehension of human emotions and values. They argue that these fundamental challenges make achieving singularity highly unlikely in the foreseeable future.

Potential Implications:

The potential implications of singularity, if it were to occur, are both exciting and daunting. Proponents envision a world where AI could solve complex problems, eradicate diseases, revolutionize industries, and enhance human life in ways we can hardly imagine. With superintelligence, AI could accelerate scientific discoveries, optimize resource allocation, and potentially solve global challenges, such as climate change and poverty.

However, there are also concerns about the risks associated with singularity. Some worry that superintelligent AI systems could become uncontrollable, making decisions that are not aligned with human values or intentions. This could pose risks to humanity's safety and well-being. The potential for job displacement and economic disruption is another concern, as singularity could lead to significant shifts in the labor market and social structures.

Ethical Considerations:

Singularity raises profound ethical questions that demand careful consideration. The development of AI systems that surpass human intelligence requires robust ethical frameworks to guide their behavior and decision-making processes. Ensuring alignment with human values, transparency, and accountability becomes crucial to prevent unintended consequences.

Additionally, the issue of AI governance becomes paramount. Policymakers and regulatory bodies must establish regulations and standards to address the potential risks and societal implications of singularity. International collaboration and cooperation are essential to foster responsible AI development and deployment on a global scale.

The Role of Human Collaboration:

While singularity raises questions about the future of human intelligence, it is important to recognize that human collaboration with AI systems can be a powerful force for positive change. Rather than viewing AI as a rival, we can embrace it as a partner that complements and enhances human capabilities. By leveraging the unique strengths of AI, such as its data processing capabilities, pattern recognition, and computational power, can empower humans to tackle complex problems more effectively. AI can assist in scientific research, medical diagnostics, and data analysis, providing valuable insights and augmenting human decision-making processes. This collaborative approach, known as human-AI synergy, harnesses the strengths of both humans and AI systems, leading to more innovative and impactful outcomes.

Human-AI Collaboration in Ethical Decision-Making:

Ethical decision-making is an area where human-AI collaboration can have a profound impact. AI systems can assist in identifying ethical dilemmas, analyzing potential consequences, and offering alternative perspectives. By incorporating diverse values, cultural nuances, and ethical frameworks, AI can support humans in making more informed and ethically sound decisions. However, the ultimate responsibility for ethical choices should rest with humans, ensuring that AI remains a tool rather than the sole arbiter of morality.

Safeguarding Human Values:

To ensure the responsible development and deployment of AI, it is crucial to safeguard human values throughout the process. This involves embedding ethical considerations into the design and training of AI systems, promoting transparency and explainability, and addressing biases and discrimination. Human oversight and accountability mechanisms should be in place to monitor and regulate AI systems to ensure that they align with human values and respect fundamental rights.

Continued Research and Ethical Discourse:

The pursuit of singularity and the potential consequences it entails require continued research, exploration, and ethical discourse. Interdisciplinary collaborations and open dialogue among scientists, ethicists, policymakers, and the public are essential to navigate the complexities and implications of singularity. Ethical review boards and expert committees can provide guidance and oversight to ensure that research and development efforts prioritize human well-being and align with societal values.

Education and Preparedness:

Preparing for the potential outcomes of singularity requires a focus on education and preparedness. Educational institutions should integrate AI literacy, ethics, and critical thinking into curricula at all levels. This will equip individuals with the knowledge and skills to navigate the evolving landscape of AI and contribute to shaping its future. Collaboration between academia, industry, and policymakers can facilitate the development of educational programs and initiatives that promote responsible AI use and foster a well-informed society.

Conclusion:

Singularity represents the ultimate frontier of AI, where the capabilities of artificial intelligence surpass human intelligence.

While the feasibility and timeline of singularity remain uncertain, the ongoing advancements in AI warrant careful consideration of its ethical, societal, and governance implications. Embracing human-AI collaboration, safeguarding human values, and promoting responsible development can maximize the potential benefits of AI while mitigating risks. By fostering interdisciplinary collaboration, ethical discourse, and education, we can shape the future of AI in a way that aligns with human values and ensures a positive impact on society. As we navigate the path towards potential singularity, it is imperative to prioritize the well-being, autonomy, and flourishing of humanity.

Chapter 21:

Beyond Human Limits: How Extraterrestrials Advanced AI Technologies

In the vast expanse of the universe, where countless civilizations thrive, it is not entirely far-fetched to imagine that some of these advanced extraterrestrial beings have played a pivotal role in propelling our own technological progress. This chapter explores the intriguing notion that aliens, with their superior knowledge and capabilities, have contributed to the development and evolution of artificial intelligence (AI) here on Earth.

While the existence of extraterrestrial life remains a subject of debate and speculation among scientists and enthusiasts alike, it is worth considering the possibility that highly advanced civilizations have been observing us for centuries, quietly influencing our technological growth from behind the scenes. Let us embark on a thought-provoking journey that explores how these cosmic entities may have catalyzed the development of AI technologies.

To comprehend the profound influence of extraterrestrials on AI, we must first acknowledge the remarkable advancements made in this field. From early computer systems to the emergence of machine learning and neural networks, AI has rapidly evolved, transforming multiple facets of our lives. However, the question arises: Could human ingenuity alone account for such exponential growth?

Believers in the extraterrestrial AI connection point to several intriguing facts that support their claims. One such fact is the so-called "Roswell Incident" in 1947, when an unidentified flying object (UFO) allegedly crashed near Roswell, New Mexico. According to some conspiracy theorists, the wreckage included advanced AI technology far beyond anything developed on Earth at the time. Could this have been an intentional extraterrestrial "gift" to accelerate our progress?

Another aspect worth considering is the sudden leaps in AI capabilities witnessed in recent decades. The rapid ascent of machine learning, natural language processing, and computer vision has left many experts astounded. Could these breakthroughs be attributed to the guidance of advanced alien civilizations?

Interestingly, throughout history, numerous accounts of close encounters and alien abductions have been reported. While skeptics dismiss them as mere fantasies or hallucinations, proponents of the extraterrestrial AI connection argue that these interactions could have served as conduits for knowledge exchange. Perhaps these encounters involved imparting profound insights on AI concepts, algorithms, and architectures, pushing our research and development efforts in unprecedented directions.

Moreover, some ufologists argue that the technological hurdles we have overcome are too significant to be solely attributed to human capabilities. The exponential growth of computing power, the development of quantum computing, and the advent of neural networks have revolutionized AI. Could these breakthroughs be the result of extraterrestrial guidance, subtly steering us towards achieving a higher level of AI intelligence?

In exploring this hypothesis, we must also consider the parallels between certain AI advancements and the capabilities attributed to extraterrestrial beings. For instance, the ability of AI systems to process vast amounts of data and make lightning-fast decisions can be compared to the supposed telepathic abilities of extraterrestrial life forms. Is it possible that our AI systems have been indirectly influenced by these superior mental processes?

Although these claims may sound fantastical, it is crucial to approach this topic with an open mind. After all, human progress has often been driven by unexpected factors and influences. If we accept the possibility of extraterrestrial intervention, it opens up exciting avenues for further exploration and understanding of the cosmos.

In conclusion, the idea that extraterrestrials have played a role in advancing AI technologies is a captivating concept.

Chapter 22:

Special Chapter - Everything You Need to Know about eBook Publishing, Book Publishing, and Audiobook Publishing through Amazon and Other Platforms Using AI

In this special chapter, we will delve into the fascinating world of publishing through digital platforms, specifically focusing on eBook publishing, book publishing, and audiobook publishing. We will explore how artificial intelligence (AI) is revolutionizing the publishing industry, making it more accessible and empowering aspiring authors and publishers like never before.

1. The Rise of Digital Publishing:

Digital publishing has transformed the way books are created, distributed, and consumed. With the advent of e-readers, tablets, and smartphones, eBooks have gained immense popularity, offering readers the convenience of accessing books anywhere, anytime. AI has played a significant role in streamlining the digital publishing process, making it easier for authors to get their work out into the world.

2. eBook Publishing Platforms:

One of the most prominent platforms for eBook publishing is Amazon Kindle Direct Publishing (KDP). KDP allows authors to self-publish their eBooks in a simple and user-friendly manner. AI algorithms employed by KDP assist authors in formatting their eBooks, creating eye-catching covers, and optimizing metadata for improved discoverability. These algorithms analyze market trends, reader preferences, and historical data to provide authors with valuable insights to enhance their book's chances of success.

3. AI Publishing Academy:

AI Publishing Academy is a notable company that utilizes AI technology to guide and support authors throughout the publishing process. They offer a comprehensive range of services, including manuscript editing, cover design, formatting, and marketing guidance. AI Publishing Academy uses natural language processing algorithms to provide authors with detailed feedback on their writing style, grammar, and overall book quality. This feedback helps authors refine their work and ensure a professional end product.

4. Print-on-Demand Publishing:

While eBooks have gained popularity, print books still hold a special place in the hearts of many readers. Print-on-demand (POD) publishing has emerged as a cost-effective solution for authors and small publishers. Companies like Amazon's CreateSpace (now merged with KDP) and IngramSpark offer POD services, allowing authors to have their books printed and shipped on demand, eliminating the need for large upfront printing costs. AI algorithms assist in print formatting, cover design, and quality control to ensure a seamless publishing experience.

5. Audiobook Publishing:

Audiobooks have witnessed a remarkable surge in popularity, with more readers embracing the audio format. With the help of AI, authors can now transform their written works into captivating audiobooks. Companies like ACX (Audiobook Creation Exchange), an Amazon subsidiary, provide a platform for authors to connect with narrators and produce high-quality audiobooks. AI-powered tools assist in audio editing, noise reduction, and audio file optimization, resulting in professional-grade audiobooks.

6. AI-Driven Book Marketing:

Once your book is published, effective marketing is crucial for reaching a wider audience. AI technologies have revolutionized book marketing strategies, enabling targeted advertising, personalized recommendations, and data-driven campaigns. Platforms like Amazon Advertising and social media platforms utilize AI algorithms to analyze user behavior, demographics, and interests, helping authors tailor their marketing efforts to the right audience. AI-powered analytics provide real-time insights on campaign performance, enabling authors to make data-driven decisions for optimal results.

7. Metadata Optimization:

Metadata plays a pivotal role in book discoverability. AI algorithms analyze keywords, book descriptions, and genre classifications to optimize metadata for maximum visibility.

Chapter 23:

Strategies for Maximum Visibility

In today's competitive landscape, maximizing visibility is essential for businesses and individuals alike. Whether you're promoting a product, building a personal brand, or trying to reach a wider audience, having a strong presence in the right places can significantly impact your success. In this chapter, we will explore various strategies and techniques for achieving maximum visibility.

1. **Define Your Target Audience:** Before implementing any visibility strategies, it's crucial to identify your target audience. Understanding who your ideal customers or followers are will help you tailor your approach and choose the most effective channels to reach them.

2. **Create High-Quality Content:** Content is king when it comes to visibility. Whether it's blog posts, videos, podcasts, or social media updates, focus on creating valuable, engaging, and shareable content that resonates with your target audience. Consistency is key, so aim to provide regular updates that keep your audience coming back for more.

3. **Leverage Search Engine Optimization (SEO):** Optimizing your online content for search engines can significantly improve your visibility. Research and incorporate relevant keywords, optimize meta tags, and ensure your website's structure is search engine friendly. High-quality backlinks

from reputable sources can also boost your visibility in search engine results.

4. **Engage in Social Media Marketing:** Social media platforms provide excellent opportunities for visibility. Identify the platforms where your target audience is most active and create a strong presence there. Engage with your audience, share your content, and participate in relevant conversations. Utilize hashtags strategically to expand your reach and consider partnering with influencers for added exposure.

5. **Guest Blogging and Influencer Collaborations:** Collaborating with influencers and guest blogging on established platforms can give you access to a wider audience. Seek out reputable blogs, podcasts, or YouTube channels in your industry and offer to provide valuable content or collaborate on a project. This can help you establish credibility and gain visibility among a larger audience.

6. **Utilize Email Marketing:** Email marketing remains one of the most effective ways to reach and engage with your audience. Build an email list by offering valuable content or incentives and regularly send out newsletters or updates to keep your subscribers informed and engaged. Personalize your emails to make them more relevant and compelling.

7. **Harness the Power of Video:** Video content continues to gain popularity and has a higher chance of going viral compared to other forms of media. Consider creating video content for platforms like YouTube, TikTok, or Instagram Reels. Be

creative, authentic, and focus on delivering value to your viewers.

8. **Collaborate and Network:** Building relationships and collaborating with others in your industry can expand your visibility. Attend industry events, join professional associations, and engage with like-minded individuals online. Collaborating on projects, hosting webinars, or participating in podcasts can help you tap into new audiences and gain credibility.

9. **Consider Paid Advertising:** While organic visibility strategies are essential, paid advertising can provide an extra boost. Platforms like Google Ads, social media ads, and influencer partnerships allow you to target specific demographics and reach a broader audience quickly. Set clear goals and monitor your campaigns to optimize results.

10. **Monitor and Analyze:** Continuously monitor your visibility efforts and analyze the data to identify what's working and what needs improvement. Tools like Google Analytics, social media insights, and SEO tools provide valuable data on your audience, engagement, and visibility metrics. Use this information to refine your strategies and make data-driven decisions.

Remember, visibility is not just about being seen; it's about creating a lasting impression and building a meaningful connection with your audience. Here are a few additional strategies to consider:

11. **Develop a Strong Personal Brand:** Building a personal brand can significantly enhance your visibility. Define your unique value proposition and communicate it consistently across all your channels. Be authentic, showcase your expertise, and establish yourself as a thought leader in your industry. This will help you stand out and attract a loyal following.

12. **Utilize Online Communities and Forums:** Engaging in relevant online communities and forums can boost your visibility among a targeted audience. Identify platforms where your audience actively participates and join the conversations. Provide valuable insights, answer questions, and establish yourself as a helpful resource. Avoid overly promotional tactics and focus on building genuine connections.

13. **Optimize for Mobile:** With the rise of mobile usage, optimizing your online presence for mobile devices is crucial for maximum visibility. Ensure your website is mobile-friendly, emails are responsive, and your content is easily consumed on smaller screens. Mobile optimization improves user experience and helps you reach a wider audience.

14. **Repurpose and Syndicate Content:** Repurposing your existing content into different formats and syndicating it across various platforms can expand your visibility. For example, transform a blog post into a podcast episode, create infographics from your data-driven articles, or turn videos into written transcripts. Syndicate your content on reputable platforms to reach new audiences and gain exposure.

15. **Participate in Speaking Engagements and Webinars:** Speaking at industry events, conferences, or webinars can significantly enhance your visibility. Share your expertise and insights with a live audience, and leverage the event's promotional efforts to reach a broader group of individuals. Engage with attendees, answer questions, and follow up with relevant resources to solidify your presence.

16. **Monitor Online Reviews and Reputation:** Online reviews and reputation can greatly impact your visibility and credibility. Monitor and respond promptly to customer reviews and feedback across various platforms. Encourage satisfied customers to leave positive reviews and address any negative feedback in a professional and helpful manner. A positive online reputation can attract new customers and improve your visibility.

17. **Collaborate with Complementary Brands**: Partnering with complementary brands or businesses can expand your visibility by tapping into each other's audiences. Look for opportunities to collaborate on joint marketing campaigns, co-create content, or cross-promote each other's products or services. This strategy allows you to reach new audiences who may be interested in what you have to offer.

18. **Develop Strategic Alliances:** Forming strategic alliances with influential individuals or organizations in your industry can significantly boost your visibility. Seek out partnerships with trusted industry leaders, influencers, or media outlets.

This can involve joint ventures, co-authoring articles or books, or featuring each other in interviews or podcasts. Strategic alliances lend credibility and help you reach a wider audience.

19. **Stay Active in Industry Trends and News:** To maintain maximum visibility, stay up to date with industry trends and news. Share your insights and opinions on relevant topics through blog posts, social media updates, or video content. Engage in discussions and provide value by offering unique perspectives. This positions you as an authority and keeps your audience engaged.

20. **Continuously Adapt and Evolve:** The digital landscape is constantly evolving, and visibility strategies that work today may become less effective tomorrow. Stay agile and adapt to emerging trends and technologies. Monitor the success of your visibility efforts, experiment with new approaches, and be willing to adjust your strategies based on data and feedback. Embrace innovation and stay ahead of the curve to maintain maximum visibility.

21. **Harness the Power of Influencer Marketing:** Influencer marketing has become a powerful tool for increasing visibility. Identify influencers in your industry whose audience aligns with your target market. Collaborate with them on sponsored content, product reviews, or endorsements. Influencers have a dedicated following that trusts their recommendations, and leveraging their influence can significantly boost your visibility.

22. **Utilize Online Advertising Platforms:** Online advertising platforms, such as Google Ads, Facebook Ads, or LinkedIn Ads, provide targeted visibility to specific demographics. Leverage these platforms to reach your ideal audience based on their interests, demographics, or online behavior. Design compelling ad campaigns with clear calls-to-action to drive traffic and increase brand visibility.

23. **Optimize for Voice Search:** With the rise of smart speakers and virtual assistants, optimizing your content for voice search is becoming increasingly important. Voice search queries often differ from typed searches, so focus on long-tail keywords, conversational language, and providing concise, direct answers to common questions. By optimizing for voice search, you can enhance your visibility in voice search results.

24. **Utilize User-Generated Content (UGC):** User-generated content is a powerful visibility tool as it involves your audience in promoting your brand. Encourage your customers or followers to create and share content related to your brand, such as testimonials, reviews, or social media posts. Repost and share user-generated content, acknowledging and rewarding your audience's participation. UGC builds trust and expands your visibility through the networks of your engaged customers.

25. **Host Webinars and Live Events:** Hosting webinars or live events allows you to connect with your audience in real-time, showcase your expertise, and increase visibility. Offer

valuable insights, engage in interactive discussions, and provide opportunities for attendees to ask questions. Promote your webinars or events through various channels to attract a wider audience and generate buzz around your brand.

26. **Collaborate with Local Businesses:** If you have a physical presence or target a specific geographic area, collaborating with local businesses can boost your visibility within the community. Partner with nearby businesses for co-marketing campaigns, sponsor local events, or participate in community initiatives. By aligning with local partners, you tap into their existing networks and gain visibility among local audiences.

27. **Implement Referral Programs:** Referral programs incentivize your existing customers or followers to refer new customers to your business. By offering rewards or discounts for successful referrals, you encourage your audience to become ambassadors for your brand. Word-of-mouth recommendations can significantly increase your visibility as people trust recommendations from their friends and peers.

28. **Monitor and Respond to Online Conversations:** Stay actively engaged in online conversations related to your industry, brand, or relevant topics. Monitor social media platforms, forums, and review sites for mentions of your brand or industry. Respond promptly and thoughtfully to both positive and negative interactions, showing that you value your audience's feedback and are committed to customer

satisfaction. Active participation in online conversations helps increase your visibility and brand reputation.

29. **Continuously Build and Nurture Relationships:** Building and nurturing relationships is a fundamental aspect of maximizing visibility. Engage with your audience, customers, and industry peers on a regular basis. Respond to comments, messages, and inquiries promptly and authentically. Show appreciation for their support and create opportunities for meaningful interactions. Strong relationships can lead to word-of-mouth promotion, collaborations, and increased visibility.

30. **Implement Influencer Outreach:** In addition to influencer collaborations, proactively reach out to influencers in your industry to expand your visibility. Research influencers who align with your brand values and target audience. Craft personalized messages highlighting how a partnership could be mutually beneficial. Offer value in exchange for their endorsement or promotion, such as exclusive content or access to your products or services.

31. **Leverage Online PR and Media Coverage:** Public relations (PR) and media coverage can significantly enhance your visibility. Develop relationships with journalists, bloggers, and industry publications. Pitch newsworthy stories, industry insights, or guest articles that align with their audience's interests. Being featured in respected media outlets can increase your credibility and expose you to a wider audience.

32. **Engage in Thought Leadership:** Establish yourself as a thought leader in your industry to boost your visibility. Share your expertise through blog posts, articles, or whitepapers. Speak at conferences, contribute to industry publications, or host webinars on relevant topics. By consistently providing valuable insights and innovative ideas, you position yourself as an authority and attract a dedicated following.

33. **Leverage the Power of Online Communities:** Join and actively participate in online communities, forums, and social media groups relevant to your industry or niche. Contribute valuable insights, answer questions, and engage in discussions. Avoid self-promotion and focus on providing value. By becoming a respected and trusted member of these communities, you increase your visibility and attract a targeted audience.

34. **Develop Strategic Content Partnerships:** Collaborate with complementary brands or content creators to amplify your visibility. Identify partners who share a similar target audience but offer different products or services. Co-create content, cross-promote each other's offerings, or run joint marketing campaigns. This strategic partnership allows you to tap into new audiences and expand your visibility.

35. **Utilize Local SEO Strategies:** If you have a physical location or target a specific geographic area, optimizing for local search is essential. Claim and optimize your Google My Business listing, ensure accurate and consistent NAP (Name, Address,

Phone Number) information across online directories, and encourage customers to leave reviews. Local SEO strategies increase your visibility in local search results and drive more foot traffic to your business.

36. **Monitor Brand Mentions:** Regularly monitor online platforms and social media for brand mentions. Use social listening tools or set up Google Alerts to stay informed about conversations related to your brand. Engage with users who mention your brand, whether it's positive or negative feedback. This proactive approach helps you address concerns, show appreciation, and maintain a positive brand image.

37. **Collaborate with Non-Competing Partners:** Seek out non-competing partners who share a similar target audience and collaborate on joint initiatives. This could include co-hosting webinars, cross-promoting each other's content, or bundling products or services. By leveraging each other's networks and resources, you can increase visibility and attract new customers.

38. **Embrace User Engagement:** Encourage user engagement across your online platforms.

Chapter 24:

Accelerating Wealth Accumulation through AI: Exploring Opportunities and Strategies

In recent years, artificial intelligence (AI) has emerged as a transformative technology with immense potential for wealth accumulation. Leveraging the power of AI in various domains can enable individuals and organizations to expedite their journey toward financial prosperity. In this chapter, we delve into the realm of AI-driven wealth accumulation and present insights, strategies, and potential avenues for leveraging AI to achieve rapid and substantial financial growth.

1.Identifying Lucrative Investment Opportunities

AI has revolutionized the investment landscape by introducing advanced algorithms capable of analyzing vast amounts of data to identify valuable insights and predict market trends. Wealth accumulation through AI involves leveraging these algorithms to make data-driven investment decisions. Machine learning models can be trained to analyze historical market data, identify patterns, and generate accurate predictions. By combining AI techniques, such as natural language processing and sentiment analysis, with market data, investors can gain a competitive edge by making informed decisions in real-time. Automated trading systems powered by AI can execute trades swiftly, capitalizing on market opportunities and maximizing returns on investment.

2.Developing AI-Powered Businesses

Another avenue for rapid wealth accumulation through AI lies in building AI-powered businesses. The integration of AI technologies across various industries has the potential to enhance operational efficiency, streamline processes, and unlock new revenue streams. By harnessing AI for tasks such as customer segmentation, personalized marketing, demand forecasting, and supply chain optimization, businesses can gain a significant competitive advantage. Startups and entrepreneurs can explore opportunities in emerging AI-driven sectors such as autonomous vehicles, healthcare diagnostics, and smart home technologies. Developing innovative AI products or services can lead to exponential growth and attract substantial investment, accelerating wealth accumulation.

3.AI-Enabled Real Estate Investment (approx. 200 words):

AI can also be leveraged to optimize real estate investment strategies. By analyzing vast amounts of data, including property prices, market trends, rental yields, and demographic information, AI algorithms can identify lucrative investment opportunities. Predictive models can estimate future property values, helping investors make informed decisions about purchasing, selling, or renting properties. AI-powered platforms can provide real-time insights on property market dynamics, enabling swift and profitable transactions. Additionally, AI can assist in property management by automating tasks such as tenant screening, rent collection, and maintenance scheduling, reducing costs and increasing efficiency.

4.Risk Management and Fraud Detection

Wealth accumulation is closely tied to effective risk management. AI can play a crucial role in identifying and mitigating risks, protecting accumulated wealth. Machine learning algorithms can analyze large datasets to detect patterns indicative of potential fraud, market volatility, or economic downturns. AI-powered risk assessment models can provide early warnings and recommendations to minimize losses. Moreover, AI can enhance cybersecurity measures, safeguarding assets from cyber threats and data breaches.

Conclusion

AI presents a wealth of opportunities for individuals and businesses to accelerate their journey towards financial prosperity. By leveraging AI to identify investment opportunities, develop AI-powered businesses, optimize real estate investments, and manage risks effectively, individuals can accumulate wealth rapidly. However, it is essential to approach AI-driven wealth accumulation with caution. Understanding the limitations and risks associated with AI, such as algorithmic biases and regulatory challenges, is crucial. Continuous learning, staying updated with technological advancements, and seeking professional advice can help navigate this dynamic landscape

Chapter 25:

THE FINAL WORD

The AI Revolution: Unleashing Wealth Accumulation in the Digital Age

"AI will have the greatest impact on our lives since the invention of the wheel." Now, before you roll your eyes and dismiss this claim as mere hyperbole, let me assure you that I am not one to spin tall tales. Well, maybe just a little, but all in good humor! The truth is, my dear reader, we are standing at the precipice of an extraordinary era where the fusion of artificial intelligence and wealth accumulation is poised to revolutionize our lives like never before.

Welcome to "The AI Revolution: Unleashing Wealth Accumulation in the Digital Age"! In this book, we embark on a delightful journey where we unravel the secrets of AI and explore how it can become your trusty ally in the quest for financial prosperity. But fret not, for this won't be a dry, monotonous read filled with jargon and endless lines of code. No, no! We're going to infuse a healthy dose of wit and charm, making your journey through this book as enjoyable as savoring a scoop of your favorite ice cream (unless you're lactose intolerant, in which case, let's go with a refreshing fruit salad).

So, why should you care about AI and wealth accumulation? Well, my friend, let me paint you a picture. Imagine having a personal assistant who can analyze mountains of financial data, spot lucrative investment opportunities, and provide you with real-time insights faster than you can say "cha-ching!" Now imagine this assistant never tires, never gets distracted by cute cat videos, and never sneaks off for a coffee break. How marvelous would that be? We're talking about a companion that can help you navigate the complex world of finance, guiding you towards the pot of gold at the end of the rainbow.

But wait, there's more! AI isn't just confined to the realm of finance. It has permeated nearly every aspect of our lives, from the way we shop, communicate, and even find love (yes, even Cupid is getting a digital upgrade). The impact of AI is akin to a technological hurricane, sweeping through industries with unprecedented force. And if you're not prepared to ride this wave, you might find yourself clinging to outdated practices while the world races ahead.

In this book, we dove into the nitty-gritty of AI and its applications in wealth accumulation. We'll demystify the buzzwords, separate fact from fiction, and equip you with the knowledge and tools to harness the immense potential of this digital powerhouse. Whether you're an aspiring investor, a seasoned entrepreneur, or simply someone fascinated by the wonders of technology, this book will open your eyes to new possibilities and empower you to make informed decisions in the ever-evolving landscape of wealth accumulation.

So, dear reader, fasten your seatbelt and prepare for an exhilarating adventure. Together, we'll explore the realms of artificial intelligence, uncover hidden treasures of financial wisdom, and embark on a journey that will revolutionize the way you think about wealth accumulation. Get ready to embrace the wondrous capabilities of AI and let it guide you toward a future filled with prosperity, possibility, and a sprinkle of whimsy. Let's embark on this grand adventure together!

www.ingramcontent.com/pod-product-compliance
Lightning Source LLC
Chambersburg PA
CBHW040758220326
41597CB00029BB/4985